Louis Wain: Catland

CATLAND

Illustrated by LOUIS WAIN

Louis Wain.

Introduced by Rodney Dale

MAGNA BOOKS

First published in 1977 by
Gerald Duckworth & Co. Ltd

Illustrations © 1977 by estate of the late Lous William Wain
Text © 1977 by Rodney A.M. Dale

This edition published 1995 by
The Promotional Reprint Company Ltd
exclusively for Magna Books, Magna Road,
Wigston, Leicester LE18 4ZH

ISBN 1 85422 922 2

Printed and bound in Hong Kong

LOUIS WAIN
by Rodney Dale

'When I was young,' said Louis Wain, 'no public man would have dared acknowledge himself a cat enthusiast; now even MPs can do so without danger of being laughed at.'

This raising of the social status of the cat was due, in no small measure, to Louis Wain himself. It was more by accident than design that the inimitable Louis Wain cat was born, but, having been born, its success was such that its procreator was hailed as an expert on cats, and found himself holding many influential positions in the Cat Fancy. He gave unstintingly of his time, money, and support and, in spite of his exceptional ideas of animal behaviour and care, Pussydom prospered. He lived to nearly eighty and, though he spent the last fifteen years of his life in mental hospitals, it was therein that much of his best work was produced.

Let us look at Louis Wain's life and art, and see how much the richer we are for it.

Louis Wain's father was William Matthew Wain, who moved to London from Leek, in Staffordshire, in his thirties. He had been converted to Roman Catholicism, and it was through the church that he met Julie Felicie Boiteux, an Anglo-French textile designer. Clearly, the two had much in common, and it was no surprise when they married in 1859.

The following year, their first child, Louis William, was born on 5 August. He was followed by five sisters, born between 1862 and 1871.

Louis was what was termed in Victorian times a 'sickly child'. In his childhood, he suffered from terrifying recurring dreams – 'visions of extraordinary complexity'. However, at the age of nine, he contracted scarlet fever and from the time of his recovery he was never again haunted by visions. He wrote that from then on, he grew 'strong and pugnacious and difficult to control'.

His somewhat erratic schooling began at the Orchard Street Foundation School in South Hackney. It appears that he played truant often, visiting the docks, museums and Woolwich Arsenal, and going off on nature rambles. From Orchard Street, he went to St Joseph's Academy, Kensington, a Roman Catholic foundation.

He had some difficulty in deciding upon a career; his 'fancy trembled in the balance between music, painting, authorship and chemistry'. Finally, at the age of seventeen, he decided to become a musician, though evidence of his success is lacking. The compositions which he frequently said he had written – which included a full-length opera – are missing, and the only account we have of his musical ability is that he played wild, *agitato* piano improvisations.

He studied music for less than a year; then decided that art would provide an easier path to fame and fortune, though he must have had some artistic talent to start with. But we have only his word for the way his career developed; later he wrote:

I might in one sense say that I have had an art training all my life, for I never contemplated being anything but an artist in one form or another.

For three years, he studied at the West London School of Art, and he stayed on as a teacher. From what we know of his shy and retiring character this could hardly have been successful, and was certainly not in itself the path to fame and fortune.

It was clear, however, that his sights were set on being a popular illustrator rather than a 'heavy' artist, and his stay at the WLSA gave him an opportunity to build up a portfolio of work to show to publishers and editors.

In 1880, his father died. This left Louis the sole male among six females; perhaps he was somewhat overpowered by the houseful of girls: perhaps he needed peace and quiet to pursue his studies. For one reason or another, he left home and worked singlemindedly at his art.

His first published drawing (*Bullfinches on the Laurels*, erroneously entitled *Robin's* [sic] *Breakfast*) appeared in the *Illustrated Sporting and Dramatic News* on 10 December 1881. The following year he gave up teaching and joined the staff of the *IS &DN* to report on animal and agricultural shows. He would travel to a show, make notes, sketch the winners after the judging, travel home, and write and illustrate his report. Since the pen is slower than the camera, the pressure on the illustrator-reporter of those days was very high.

Although he needed solitude, he did not cut himself off from his family completely, particularly since the arrival of his sisters' governess, Emily Richardson. She was ten years older than he; nevertheless, they fell in love. went to live together, and then married in Hampstead on 30 January 1884 – Louis' twenty-fourth year.

Their happiness was short-lived. Emily was found to have cancer of the breast, and was soon confined to her bed. One of the diversions she had was a black and white kitten called Peter (1882–1898), and Louis would sit sketching him in all postures, hour after hour, to amuse Emily. She wanted him to show his cat drawings to the editors for whom he worked, but he feared that they would detract from his 'serious' illustration. When at last he did venture to show some, the comment was: 'Whoever would want to see a picture of a cat?' That was the end of that for the time being.

Sir William Ingram, proprietor of the *Illustrated London News*, thought differently. Wain had shown him some drawings including cats; Sir William published one or two of them and from then on kept a friendly eye on the young artist. The break came in 1886. In that year, Wain drew some kitten illustrations for a children's book, *Madame Tabby's Establishment*. And that Christmas, Sir William commissioned a double-page narrative drawing for the *ILN*, 'A Kittens' Christmas Party'. It took Louis Wain eleven days to draw, and contains some 200 cats (though some are very sketchy). But it was an immediate success. According to Wain, it brought him 'overnight fame, and enquiries from all over the world'. For the next quarter of a century, he was never short of a commission.

Emily had little opportunity to share in her husband's sudden fortune; after long suffering, she died on 2 January 1887.

Louis Wain did not allow himself to become brooding and mournful. Emily's death was, after all, a 'merciful release', and his mind was diverted by the mounting demand for his work.

At this stage, he was still a general illustrator who had won some acclaim for a narrative drawing of kittens. There was some resistance towards an artist who specialised in this sort of work. Nevertheless, he had so many studies of Peter that the idea of 'working them up', as he put it, was obviously an attractive one.

Indeed, in the 'Christmas Party' we see the beginnings of the Louis Wain cat, in the feline band which accompanies the dancing. Time went on; the cats became more and more involved in human pursuits, while remaining firmly catlike. Then came the transition, in about 1890. The cats began to walk on their hind legs, don fancy neckwear, and sport monocles and walking-sticks – the Louis Wain cat had been born.

As Louis Wain cats developed, they became more and more uncatlike in their behaviour, and more and more like naughty (or ingenious)

1. Moonlight Sonata

children. But they were still undoubtedly cats. All the cats in this book somehow remain plausible, whatever they are doing. Certainly anyone who knows cats well will constantly see their Louis Wain-ness breaking through – it takes little imagination for a Wainophile to see his cat sloping off for a round of golf or a quick plunge in the briny.

So, from the 1890s, Louis Wain cats appear in action-packed panoramas, sometimes dozens of them in running battle with one another or with the dogs, the ghastly outcome of which can only be conjectured. His skill in conveying expression on the cats' faces is astonishing – in *Diabolo* [3] we see the whole range: surprise, concentration, frustration – and more.

Very seldom are the cats represented as caricatures of humans. *My Friend the Prince* [9] is the exception in this book, and shows how devastating Louis Wain could be if he so wished.

One factor, not immediately apparent, which helps to make the Louis Wain cat credible, is its lack of clothes: when a Louis Wain cat wears clothes it is to underline some point in the picture. In the majority of the plates in this book the cats are unclothed. However, in *The Naughty Puss* [5] there is no doubt that the central figure, the one in charge, is the one with the frilly bonnet. In *My Friend the Prince* [9], the clothes are needed to emphasise the shapes of the cats – especially the ladies. In *Seaside Joys* [7] the kittens are wearing bathing trunks to underline the seasideness of the scene. In *Moonlight Sonata* [1] the 'cat boys' need clothes to make their presence among the birds credible. By contrast, in such scenes as *Diabolo* [3] no clothes are needed, so there are none.

Louis Wain took little notice of the anatomy of the cat – probably it is as well that he did not, for he might then have found himself unable to draw some of the postures that he did. A critical and perceptive child once said 'Mummy, they aren't cats, they haven't any bones'. That child was right; so many Louis Wain cats have india-rubber limbs and bodies, arranged as the picture demands with a breathtaking disregard for

accuracy. *Orpheus* [13] and *We Said We Were Playing Golf* [6] are but two examples in this collection illustrating the bending of the anatomy to the demands of the subject.

As we have seen, Louis Wain's object was not primarily to satirise either cats or humans: if there is satire in his pictures, it is usually incidental. His humour was straightforward, boisterous and Victorian. He wanted a vehicle for his playfulness, and for one reason or another chose the cat, in much the same way as W. Heath Robinson found mechanical engineering a convenient peg on which to hang *his* playfulness.

It is, of course, tempting to speculate that Louis Wain was obsessed with cats because of Peter's association with Emily's terminal illness. However, such speculation overlooks the wide variety of other subjects he illustrated, an example of which we see here in *Moonlight Sonata* [1]. I lend little credence to the story that he once confided to a friend that his late wife's soul had taken over Peter on her death.

But to return to the Louis Wain cat – the animal which conferred upon its inventor a fame of the sort today accorded to a television personality (often with far less ability than Louis Wain). This fame also gave him the false authority which goes with the breed. Because he drew cats, he must be an expert on them: accordingly, within five years of his *ILN* drawing, he found himself President of the National Cat Club, and many similar honours were to follow.

In that same year (1891), he was thought of so highly that he was mentioned in a book about the Dutch cat artist, Henriette Ronner (1821–1909), as being one of the few Englishmen 'who understand and appreciate feline beauty and feline character', though admittedly he was 'not of the character of Madame Ronner'. Ronner's compositions are suitable for chocolate-boxes, though her technique elevates her above that genre. Louis Wain admired her immensely, and copied at least one of her kitten drawings stroke by stroke.

Louis Wain.

2. Love at First Sight

CATLAND

However, honoured as he may have been, an expert on cats he definitely was not: he held distinctly strange ideas about them and their treatment. For example, he wrote of the cat:

Here is an animal whose brain is in a transitory condition of development, whose sensorium in most specimens is not in a condition to withstand the shock of rapidly changing impressions without a severe mental strain which immediately reacts on the digestive organs. As a consequence, the cat will cling to the original home, to the set of impressions the sensory nerve is most used to convey to the mind without effort, while it will suffer severe and obvious distress to the sensory organs when the sight is made to convey a number of strange and unusual scenes to them. The digestion suffers, the cat cannot eat well, and very often dies before the brain can recover its equilibrium.

This frailty of the cat's brain, however, has its uses. For example, when asked how it was that cats found their way home over incredible distances (and the truth of *that* belief is by no means irrefutable) Louis Wain replied that:

the goal is so strongly impressed on the cat's brain that it is able to reason out its means and methods in order to reach it.

He continued:

Strangely enough, I once had the impression that a cat's tendency was to travel north, and to face north as a magnet does, and that this tendency had some intimate association with the electrical strength of its fur.

Louis Wain was perhaps thinking of the electrical strength of the fur when he drew *The Fire of the Mind Agitates the Atmosphere* [11] some thirty years later.

There are numerous other examples of his novel cat theories, but these will suffice for the present. It will not be surprising to find that Wain's ideas on other scientific topics were equally at variance with those commonly held. Although he said that he had 'studied the physical sciences', his drawings belie this. We have a good example here if we look at the wheels of the rickshaw in *Love at First Sight* [2]. How *are* they fixed on?

He often said that he was working on 'several inventions' that he was patenting, but the records show three only, and they are provisional – that being so, we shall never know their details. His scientific studies are, in the main, just a part of his fantasy world. The life that he was living in the mid-1890s was sheer hard work. However, we have seen that Sir William Ingram had taken an interest in Louis Wain, and it was no doubt he, who owned property at Westgate-on-Sea (near Margate), who suggested that the Wain family might move to that town and be re-united.

Louis was a keen sportsman, specialising in boxing (he had been a pupil of the pugilist Jem Mace), fencing and athletics. He even went so far as to name two of the three houses in which they lived consecutively at Westgate 'Bendigo Lodge', after the prizefighter 'Bendigo' (William Thompson 1811–1880) whom he much admired.

Having established himself as an artist, there was no need for Louis Wain to work quite so frantically, and he made the most of the opportunities offered by Westgate for swimming, fishing, and boating. Sir William Ingram deserves our thanks for the help he undoubtedly gave the Wains.

By now, the Louis Wain cat was fully developed, and such works as *The Good Puss* [4] and *The Naughty Puss* [5] were well-known, and hanging in many nurseries – they were reproduced by the hundred.

In *The Naughty Puss*, we see the stylised Dame School, with slates, dunce in the corner, and a portrait of Our Founder (presumably), General Catty, looking sternly down at the scene. All the down-to-earth jokes are there – 'Miss Catty is a

3. Diabolo

4. The Good Puss

5. The Naughty Puss

rat' written on the slate (hence the chastisement), and the map of Cattyland on the wall, divided into such provinces as Catsupshire, Mouseyshire, Tabbyshire and Manx Island. This pair of works also offers several examples of Louis Wain's slapdash lettering. He never did learn calligraphy, and much of his work is the worse for it. Pieces such as *Catland*, the cover of this book, were lettered by another hand.

Although an artist, Louis Wain was always a journalist: his work was often topical, and crazes and events were reflected in the doings of his cats. Two examples are shown here: *Diabolo* [3] and *Love at First Sight* [2]. Diabolo was a craze which suddenly emerged in 1907. And why are the cats in *Love at First Sight* Japanese? Because of the Japan-British exhibition held in 1910.

Come, Birdie, Come [8] was a perennial theme of Wain's, based on C. A. White's very popular ballad of that title (1874):

> Beautiful bird of spring has come
> Seeking a place to build his home
> Warbling his song so light and free
> Beautiful bird, come live with me ...
>   We will be happy, light and free
>   You shall be all the world to me
>   Come birdie come and live with me ...

Just the song for a Louis Wain cat.

There is no doubt of the popularity of Louis Wain's work. In *The Book of the Cat* (1903), Frances Simpson wrote:

In these latter days, who is there amongst us, young and old, who has not enjoyed a hearty laugh over the comical cats of Louis Wain? In his particular line, he is unique, for no one has ever portrayed cats in such various attitudes and with such deliciously expressive countenances. The adjectives and adverbs of the Cataract of Lodore would not suffice to describe the varied emotions of these funny felines. A Christmas without one of Louis

Wain's clever catty pictures would be like a Christmas pudding without currants.

Between 1895 and 1905, some forty books illustrated by Louis Wain appeared, many written by him as well. In the first few years of this century he produced several hundred postcards. Why did his fortunes decline when he would seem to be in his prime?

Louis Wain's downfall seems to have been his shyness, kindly nature and lack of business acumen. He sold his drawings outright, and was too diffident to negotiate the fees or royalties which he could have commanded. As a result, by 1907, although he was at the height of his fame, paradoxically he had the utmost difficulty in selling his work because there was so much of it already in circulation. In that year, he was sued for debt, and judgment was entered against him. There was one way to try to redeem his fortune – to sail for a land where he would receive the welcome he deserved – America.

There, he worked for the Hearst Newspapers, drawing comic strips for three years. He seems, from his reports, to have been very impressed with America, and its Cat Fancy, and the American Cat Fancy was very impressed with Louis Wain.

In 1910, his mother died, and he returned to Westgate. Now, there were four sisters, for Marie (who died in 1913) was in a local mental hospital. Caroline and Josephine kept house; Felicie and Claire, who had had art training, discreetly pursued their work, though there was little fear of their eclipsing their brother's fame. Fame, but not fortune. His return to this country found him as poor as when he had left: apparently, he invested all his savings in a wonderful oil lamp, which used hardly any fuel. The story goes that he returned resolved to patent and exploit the invention, but the war intervened. However, there is no record of his having attempted to patent anything, and he had some four years in which to do it.

In 1914, he modelled some 'futurist' porcelain cats – they are some of the most hideous things

6. We Said We Were Playing Golf

he ever produced. The story goes that a boatload of these was torpedoed on its way to America – sad for Louis Wain, but no great loss to art. According to one reviewer:

The futurist cat is the latest thing in freak ornaments. It has been evolved from the fertile brain of Mr Louis Wain, the inimitable cat expert, whose idea of applying the tenets of futurism to the construction of china cats has resulted in the creation of some truly wonderful feline fancies . . . It can truly be said at once that if not exactly things of beauty, they are a joy for ever.

Yellow cats and blue cats, green cats and pink cats, and even pale heliotrope cats, were grouped on futurist shelves, and they were the quaintest, oddest tribe imaginable. Their faces, designed on crude cube lines, were the limit of grotesqueness, and were calculated to draw a laugh from the most miserable of men.

Today, even the least miserable of men tends to shudder. The set contained four cats, two dogs, two pigs and one 'grotesque'.

The First World War continued, and the Wains became poorer and poorer. Louis paid endless bills with his drawings, and many children and grandchildren of his creditors cherish his work today. There is no doubt that Louis Wain's private life was a great deal unhappier than his comical cats would seem to indicate. His lack of business acumen, leading to chronic shortage of cash, had been a constant source of worry – after all, he had four sisters to support.

He was a famous man in his mid-fifties, a man whose work no one wanted except out of kindness. Any money he had made in America had gone on the lamp, or sunk – literally – with the china cats.

In 1914, he lay unconscious in Bart's Hospital for a week after falling from a bus in Bond Street. His fame was such that bulletins on his progress appeared in *The Times*. The legend was that the fall had been caused by the bus swerving to avoid – a cat. The war brought with it a shortage of paper so that fewer books were published. Louis Wain's career was apparently drawing to a close.

However, in 1916, he was approached by H. D. Wood, the British film pioneer, who asked him if he would draw an animated cartoon: *Pussyfoot*. He tried hard, but the venture was not a success; although he was a lightning sketcher, that facility is not necessarily what is needed for animated drawings. The cartoon which survives is about a boy and his dog – the possible pleasure of seeing a Louis Wain cat in action is denied to us.

In 1917, the Wain family moved from Westgate back to London; 41 Brondesbury Road, Kilburn. Shortly afterwards, Caroline died in the virulent influenza epidemic of that year. This loss affected Louis very deeply.

His reputation as an eccentric probably masked from his family and friends that his mind was failing. Friends became suspicious when he started canvassing their help for a non-existent cat show he said he was organising, and talking of his scheme for breeding spotted cats.

Then his delusions became more sinister – he believed that his surviving sisters had been responsible for Caroline's death, that they were stealing his cheques, robbing him, selling his possessions. Groups of spirits, he thought, were projecting currents so that he became full of electricity. He shut himself up in his room, writing frenziedly of his electrical and spiritualistic theories. He started to move the furniture about endlessly, believing that, by doing so, he would prevent its being taken away.

He became violent and attacked his sisters, they called for the doctor, and Louis Wain was certified insane on 16 June 1924. He was taken to the pauper ward of Springfield Hospital, Tooting. There, he was noted as being a man 'of a great many eccentricities, and possessed of many quite fantastic delusions'. However, he

7. Seaside Joys

soon started to draw and paint: perhaps the rigours of the pauper asylum were a welcome change from the pressures of creditors and domestic responsibilities.

The diagnosis was schizophrenia. We do not have space here to delve deeply into that condition; suffice it to say that all we know of Louis Wain's behaviour is consistent with the diagnosis. His childhood and adolescent fantasies; his fads, fancies and obsessions; his style of writing and his art; all are indicative of a schizoid personality, which finally ruled his life to such an extent that he had to be restrained.

His sisters sorted out his affairs as best they could, and started to capitalise on their own talents. Josephine ran the household: Claire and Felicie gave sketching-lessons, and produced some very attractive glass-paintings, fore-edge paintings (on books), and miniatures. Every week they visited Louis, to take him materials and collect finished work for sale.

When Louis Wain had been at Springfield for just over a year, Dan Rider, the bookseller, who was also an asylum visitor, earned his immortality by 'discovering' Louis Wain. This 'Dr Livingstone, I presume' story bears retelling. Rider wrote:

I was on a committee that had to make a number of visits to asylums. During one of those visits, I was passing up and down a corridor when I noticed a quiet little man drawing cats. I went to inspect his work.

'Good Lord, man, you draw like Louis Wain.'

'I am Louis Wain,' replied the patient.

'You're not, you know.' I exclaimed.

'But I am,' said the artist, and he was.

Plenty of people must have known that Louis Wain was there, but it was Rider's flair for publicity which enabled him to whip up the support needed and start a fund, so that within a week Louis had been transferred to a private room at Bethlem, with the attendant comforts of a rediscovered celebrity – many people were surprised to find that he was still alive, since he had produced little published work in the previous decade.

Ramsay MacDonald, then Prime Minister, took a personal interest in the plight of the Wains – not only Louis, but his impoverished sisters. In his appeal for funds, he said:

Louis Wain was on all our walls fifteen to twenty years ago. Probably no artist has given a greater number of young people pleasure than he has.

And in a later appeal, H. G. Wells wrote:

He invented a cat style, a cat society, a whole cat world. English cats that do not look like Louis Wain cats are ashamed of themselves.

Sufficient funds were raised, and sufficient attention drawn to Wain's condition, for him to live in surroundings conducive to his starting to draw and paint again. (Further funds were forthcoming from exhibitions held in 1931 and 1937.)

The work which he was now producing in hospital differed from the hastily-produced cats for which he was, perhaps, chiefly remembered. He executed much work in watercolour and crayon, the colours became more exciting – sometimes to the point of crudity – and the ideas more daring.

In the past, there had been a series of stock poses which we can see in this collection by comparing, for example, the adult cat of *Catland* [title page] with the singing cat of *Come, Birdie, Come* [8]. Now we see some fine examples of Wain's new work. *Orpheus* [13] shows an unmistakable Louis Wain cat in a beautiful spring garden, playing the guitar to a half-circle of birds. There are twelve birds (disciples?) in the audience: this has been remarked in other works of the period.

Next, we come to *We Said We Were Playing Golf* [6]. Although this picture 'works' well, the relative proportions of cats, cattle, and the rest are, on examination, reminiscent of Hogarth's

8. Come, Birdie, Come

CATLAND

False Perspective. 'We said we were playing golf' – to whom did we say it? Our wives? Why is having a picnic less acceptable than having a round of golf?

In the background is one of the strange architectural creations which Louis Wain seemed to work into most of his out-door pictures of the period. Perhaps the most interesting feature of the picture, which we have noted time and again, is the way that the cats retain their credibility while looking as no real cats can – all are anatomically unsound, and two are bright blue. The cat in the middle is sitting as one would presumably have to sit if one had a tail – the one on the right, however, would find the position more awkward. Two appear to have overcome the problem by sitting on boxes – in practice, this would be no help at all.

The opposable thumb, the factor which has allowed the primates to rise above the rest of the animal kingdom, is here given to the cat world, allowing our subjects to hold things in an impossible, yet entirely credible, way.

It is interesting that one of the items on the menu (where is the teapot, where are the cups?) is oranges. Louis Wain loved oranges, and friends and admirers sent them to him in hospital. But one of his theories had been:

> If you don't want puss to go near any given place, put orange-peel near this place. Cats will seldom scratch up any flower at the root of which the peel is put, and I have many a time known when they would not even cross a garden wall on top of which was a continuous line of peel.

In 1967, the late Tiggy McCrow and I conducted an experiment which seemed to refute this theory, and came to the conclusion that Louis Wain's cats, when sitting on his lap, would have found an aversion from the fine natural aerosol resulting from the peeling of the oranges he loved.

From the same period as the golfing cats comes *The Fire of the Mind Agitates the Atmosphere* [11].

This is an exceedingly powerful picture: brown swirls emanate from the cats like the lines of force from magnets, made visible by means of iron filings. The cat on the left is clearly exercising an influence on the one on the right – and judging from the latter's expression, that influence is not beneficial. Perhaps this was a reflection of the artist's view of the world, that his body was charged with electricity, that ether – the source of all evil – was present in his food, that he was filled with electricity and had magic powers of healing by the laying on of hands.

Another example from these later years is *Wallpaper Cat* [10]. There is some controversy surrounding these wallpaper cats, of which he drew many. Simply, it has been asserted that the complexity of the wallpaper, coupled with the deterioration of the cat (an advanced example of this is not shown here) correlated with Louis Wain's mental state at the time the drawing was made.

Certainly, we know that the filling of pictures with detailed designs is, in some cases, a manifestation of schizophrenia. There is no doubt that the artist's deterioration was more advanced when he drew *Wallpaper Cat* than it was when he drew *Come, Birdie, Come* [8], for example. But what other factors might there have been?

Louis Wain's mother, we know, was a very talented designer of tapestries and fabrics. The initial design sketches for such works may be made on some sort of grid, and I have seen unfinished wallpaper studies of Wain's built up in fearful symmetry on carefully drawn grids. It seems to me at least as reasonable to suppose that Louis Wain was experimenting with the patterns which he remembered from his youth as that he was deteriorating.

One other possibility remains which I haven't mentioned before – Louis Wain was ambidextrous (though he usually drew left-handed), and could mirror-write fluently. The art of drawing symmetrically using both hands is not difficult to acquire, and this technique may be the origin of some of these drawings.

One example from this period remains: *The*

9. My Friend the Prince

Perfect Cat [14]. Here, the rich decoration is most pronounced. Of this 'reddish-brown creature, mainly cat and part hare', Brian Reade writes:

> Around this conception of a *perfect cat* there spreads some dream-like foliage made the more vivid by the introduction of lilac shades amidst the green. In the background there is indicated the Alhambra in Spain. This place had a special significance because numerous cats were given a home there at the time, and Wain had published a drawing of it in the 1921 Annual, with the caption 'It is now the Cats' Palace'.

On the reverse of *The Perfect Cat* is an inscription in Wain's hand typical of his schizophrenic ramblings:

> The solitary one more real persian cat is the one that is now going to be the one that is the real living animal left alone until the call is given to it at night time this evening at the same time as the rabbit can be again put to the test. This can be done by giving the call directly the light is seen after the first sleep is over . . . It is the perfect cat made the more perfect by the willingness given to it. The whole is the old time rabbit and this has now the greater life given to it to be. The deer too can now be the same in the same way.

In May 1930, Louis Wain was moved to Napsbury Hospital, near St Albans. The buildings there are set in very spacious gardens, and, although it took him some time to settle down, the doctors and nurses made life as pleasant as they could for him, and he received many visitors. He rewarded them with countless drawings, still treasured today.

Louis Wain at Napsbury was not easy to communicate with, but his art was of as high a standard as it ever had been. At Christmas, he delighted in decorating the wards, and the custom arose of his decorating the ward mirrors. *Three Singing Cats* [12] is such a work, now protected with glass, and preserved in the Guttmann Maclay collection.

His sisters continued to visit, bringing comforts, and taking work away. *Louis Wain's Great Big Midget Book* was published in 1935, but the material had appeared elsewhere, some of it dating back to the beginning of the century. The sisters were still able to support themselves in various ways with their art – for many years Claire demonstrated at exhibitions for the Royal Sovereign Pencil Co, drawing beautiful land- and seascapes to show off the different hardnesses of lead.

In November 1936, Louis Wain suffered a stroke which affected his speech and the right side of his body; in a few days, however, he was able to write with both hands, and drew a very good cat, using his left hand.

Josephine died at the beginning of 1939. Louis was not told, though he did ask why she had stopped sending him notes. However, the deception did not have to be carried on for long. By May, Louis was confined to his bed, incoherent and isolated. On 4 July 1939, he died of kidney failure and arteriosclerosis.

His body was taken to the Church of the Sacred Heart, Quex Road, Kilburn; the following day Mass was said, and he was buried at St Mary's Roman Catholic Cemetery, Kensal Green, with his father and two of his sisters. Felicie joined them within a year, and Claire in 1945.

A memorial exhibition of Louis Wain's work was held in September 1939. The critic of *The Times* unwittingly wrote Wain's epitaph:

> As a man who gave simple pleasure to thousands, Mr Wain deserves to be remembered.

But September 1939 was not a propitious time for memorial exhibitions – the world had other things on its mind, and when it had recovered, Louis Wain was forgotten. Forgotten, that is, as a public figure.

10. Wallpaper Cat

CATLAND

Many private memories of him, and his works, were treasured by many thousands of people, lying dormant until the time was right for a revival.

In 1968, my *Louis Wain: The Man Who Drew Cats* was published. I was surprised to find that I was writing the first full-length biography of the artist, and gratified, not only for myself but also for Louis Wain, at the interest it aroused. The Victoria and Albert Museum held an exhibition in the Christmas season 1972–1973, the largest collection of Louis Wain's work ever assembled. Concurrent with this was the publication of Brian Reade's excellent monograph on Louis Wain, putting the artist and his art into historical perspective.

Now, nearly forty years after Louis Wain's death, we have this collection of colour plates, under an hitherto unused cover which he designed at the turn of the century. He who was an adulated nine-days' wonder in his own time, and then forgotten for a generation, has now re-emerged with a solid reputation, properly based on some of his finest and most thoughtful work, rather than on the hasty sketches for which he was better known in his prime.

11. The Fire of the Mind Agitates the Atmosphere

Chronology

12. Three Singing Cats

1896	Member of committee of Our Dumb Friends' League
1898	Peter dies
1900	Marie certified insane
1901	First *Louis Wain Annual* published
1902	Honorary secretary to the Earl of Mar's Coronation March Song Competition
1903	'The Kit-Cats' in *The Lady's Magazine*
1907	Sails for New York (12 Oct)
1910	Mother dies aged 77 (26 Jan)
1910	Louis Wain returns from America
1913	Marie dies
1914	Produces 9 china futurist mascot cats Falls off a bus in Bond Street (7 Oct)
1915	Patents 'rangefinders'
1916	Member of Anti-vivisectionist Society Cinema cartoons
1917	Caroline dies Wains leave Westgate for Brondesbury
1921	9 more futurist mascot cats
1924	Louis Wain certified insane (16 June) Moves to Springfield Hospital
1925	'Discovered': moves to Bethlem
1930	Moves to Napsbury
1931	Exhibition at XXI Gallery
1936	Suffers a stroke (20 Nov)
1937	Exhibition at Clarendon House
1939	Josephine dies Louis Wain dies (4 July) Memorial Exhibition held (Sept)
1940	Felicie dies
1945	Claire dies

13. Orpheus

Illustrations

14. The Perfect Cat

Acknowledgments

Orpheus and *The Perfect Cat* are reproduced by permission of Brian Reade; *We Said We Were Playing Golf, Wallpaper Cat, The Fire of the Mind* and *Come, Birdie, Come* by permission of Rodney Dale; *The Good Puss* and *The Naughty Puss* by permission of Lionel Lambourne; *Three Singing Cats* by permission of the Guttmann Maclay Collection, Institute of Psychiatry; and *Catland, Moonlight Sonata, Love at First Sight, Diabolo, Seaside Joys* and *My Friend the Prince* by permission of the Victoria and Albert Museum.